Rhyming with God

Rhyming with God

Poetic Prayers & Reflections

PENNY A. POWELL

RESOURCE *Publications* • Eugene, Oregon

RHYMING WITH GOD
Poetic Prayers & Reflections

Resource Publications
An Imprint of Wipf and Stock Publishers
199 W. 8th Ave., Suite 3
Eugene, OR 97401

www.wipfandstock.com

PAPERBACK ISBN: 979-8-3852-3549-0
HARDCOVER ISBN: 979-8-3852-3550-6
EBOOK ISBN: 979-8-3852-3551-3

02/04/25

All photographs are under the author's copyright.

The author can be contacted at PennyAPowell@yahoo.com.

To my 4 C's:

Caroline, my mom
Collin, my husband
Caleb, my son
And my *caring* mother-in-law, Gloria.

My heart cannot fully express what it wants to say
But please know how much
God and I love you each and every day!

Contents

Preface   xi

Acknowledgments   xv

Enter the Room   1

My Tears Are the Cries of My Ancestors   3

Temple of the Holy Spirit   5

Poetic Movement, Embodied Worship, Devotion in Motion   7

On the Mat   8

Thank You, Jesus   9

Letting Go   10

Dear Ever-Present God   11

Dear Loving God   13

Dear Poetic God   14

Dear Radiant One   16

Bold in Christ   18

Poetic Workouts   19

Camp Gladiator   21

Poetic Encounters with "The Time ReDesign"   22

Slowing Down with God   23

Dear Nourishing God   24

Who Am I being? Who Am I becoming?   25

Slowing Down the Breath   27

Anchor   29

Sacred Word Breathing   30

Contents

The Impact of Thoughts on Time   31

Resurrection Weekend 2023   33

Don't Lose Sight of God's Love   36

Simple Poetic Prayers from my Journal   38

Rest & Reset   38

Dear Healing God   40

Devotional Writer   41

Family Tributes   42

Poetic Motherhood   44

Dear Son   45

Dear Daddy   48

Working and Flowing with God's Direction   51

Gratitude   52

My Why   55

What Am I to Do?   56

Prayers for the Prison Fellowship Ministry   58

Bittersweet: A Devotion   61

Bibliography   63

Dear God,
Thank you for these poetic prayers and reflections
May they inspire introspection for the reader
And a deep connection with You!

Please guide each mind
To seek and find
Your loving presence
And joyful essence!

In Jesus' Name,
Amen.

I, Penny, write not to impress
But rather to, prayerfully, bless
The soul of the reader
And the spirit within
Writing to express the love of God
And my love for Him!

I thank Him
And praise Him
I write in His Name
Because life in Jesus
Never leaves us the same.

Not pushing my beliefs
Simply sharing my passion
Because life in Jesus
Is my ultimate expression!

*"We have become his poetry, a re-created people that will fulfill
the destiny he has given each of us, for we are joined to Jesus, the
Anointed One. Even before we were born, God planned in advance
our destiny and the good works we would do to fulfill it."*
Ephesians 2:10 (TPT)

Preface

I have enjoyed the rhythm of rhyming poetry for as long as I can remember. I recall the collection of books written in rhyme on my childhood bookshelves. I also fondly remember a high school English teacher, Ms. Levyette (Furbert) Robinson, approaching me one day after class to say how much she enjoyed reading my "Unity" poem, which I had written as a class assignment. Amongst my writings, I also have a simple collection of non-published family-related poetry I wrote over thirty years ago as a tribute to various family members.

During the beginning of the COVID-19 pandemic, poetic prayers began pouring out of me, and they haven't stopped. Because of how easily my pen glides across the page or how quickly my fingers move across the keyboard when I'm poetically speaking with God, it's clear to me that He gives me the words to express back to Him. His words enter my spirit, and I relish documenting them. It all happens so quickly. Some mornings, a verse is even awaiting me in my mind when I awake, so I jump out of bed to write it down. I love communicating with God this way. It's fun and exhilarating. "It's our thing," I often say. "It's one of our love languages."

In the article "God Filled Your Bible with Poems" by John Piper, Leland Ryken says, "Whole books of the Bible are poetic: Job, Psalms, Proverbs, Song of Solomon. A majority of Old Testament prophecy is poetic in form. Jesus is one of the most famous poets in the world. Beyond these predominantly poetic parts of the Bible, figurative language appears throughout the Bible, and whenever it does, it requires the same type of analysis given to poetry."

Piper adds, "That is a lot of poetry—language that is chosen and structured differently from ordinary prose. God can raise the dead by any means that he pleases. He can waken dull hearts to the reality of his beauty in any way he desires. And one of the ways he pleases to do it is by inspiring his spokesmen to write poetry."[1]

Although my poetry is expressed far simpler than God's Word, writing poetic prayers helps me feel close to my creative Creator and fills me with joy. Rhyming with God is, therefore, a compilation of words to me from God that have unfolded in the form of poetic prayers and reflections. To compile them for this book, I've had to pull from pages of devotional books and journals I've written in, and computer documents I've saved. Organizing these writings into one place has been more time-consuming than composing them.

Some newer prayers and reflections arose during this organizational process, so they are also included. A bonus devotion article has been added at the end of the book, as it is part of the story that a portion of the poetry tells.

The thirty poetic expressions in this book can carry us through a month—the number God put on my heart when pondering how many poems to place within these pages. The number thirty is also symbolic of Jesus' age when beginning His ministry. And, at age thirty, I became a mother to my now-grown son, Caleb. So, the number thirty is special to my heart and soul.

I hope you will customize these thirty poems to your life. May they inspire you to compose prayers and writings of your own.

Enjoy connecting with God in this simple way! I believe He delights in us when we approach Him with the humility of a child, as we're taught to do in Matthew 18:4 (NLT)—"So anyone who becomes as humble as this little child is the greatest in the Kingdom of Heaven."

May we, therefore, humbly approach our Creator with childlike hearts and open minds, creatively expanding our prayer life with Him. In doing so, I pray that you encounter your unique rhythm that you'll come to know as your thing and your love language with God.

---

1. Piper, "God Filled Your Bible with Poems," paras. 5–6.

PREFACE

Simply take it a breath, a word, and a prayer at a time!

With Love & Poetry,

Penny A. Powell

Acknowledgments

Special thanks to:

My beloved Creator, who guides my pen. It's on His love and guidance I depend. God, I will forever love and thank You. In Jesus' Name, Amen.

My beloved family: I love you dearly and thank God with my heart and soul for each of you. There are many reasons to thank you. Love you always!

- *My husband, Collin, and our son, Caleb. Our little family of three means beyond the world to me. My love for you is eternal. Love, Love!*

- *My mother, mother-in-law/love, siblings and siblings-in-law/ love, aunts, uncles, cousins, nieces/great-nieces, nephews/great-nephews, godparents, and family friends, such as James Howard, my "brother from another mother." Jimmy, heartfelt thanks for being a constant encourager and supporter of my poetry and my life in Christ.*

- *My loved ones who gained their wings (dad, grandparents, aunts, uncles, cousins, and family friends). Your love and lessons significantly impacted my life and continue to bless me.*

My beloved friends: Thank you for your presence in my life— whether we are near or far and in contact often or not. Regarding Rhyming with God and/or the Christ-centered stretching class I teach, special thanks to:

ACKNOWLEDGMENTS

- *My BFFL (best friend for life) and walking sunflower, Teeshalavone Jenkins, for reminding me that I had written "Temple of the Holy Spirit." Otherwise, I would have overlooked including it here on page 5.*

- *My Camp Gladiator (CG) trainer and dear friend, Terie Wanger, for impacting my life through your unwavering commitment to CG members/family! "Camp Gladiator" on page 21 was inspired by your fun, beneficial workouts.*

- *My longtime island-girl "sis-star" friend from Bermuda, Keitha Binns, who mailed and surprised me with a copy of the prayer journal, Women Finding God. I initially penned "Rest & Reset" in that journal on December 22, 2021, and it is now included in Rhyming with God on page 38.*

- *My island-girl friend in Fleming Island, Florida, Anita Scarnecchia, who has spent many hours by the river with me diving into cherished conversations about life in God. That time always feels like we are rhyming with God.*

- *My sweet Bermudian, Florida-based friend, Carmen Mitchell, for graciously providing the candles from your personal collection at a moment's notice for the impromptu photoshoot by Javi Fernandez at Dance4Life. One of the photos is included in "Poetic Movement, Embodied Worship, Devotion in Motion" on page 7.*

- *My special friends in my community for supporting the embodied movement class I teach—Stretch, Strengthen, and Relax (SSR). Thank you, Laurel New (whom I met when our now-adult sons were in kindergarten), for hosting SSR since 2013.*

- *My sister in Christ, "spiritual advisor," and creator of The Time ReDesign, Etta Hornsteiner. Etta, I greatly appreciate your deep understanding of my heart for God and for inspiring "Poetic Encounters with The Time ReDesign" on page 22. Your programs that help to spiritually navigate time and liminal spaces have blessed me beyond words. Also, heartfelt thanks for introducing me to Betty M. Rolle, editor of Rhyming with God.*

- *Thank you, Betty, for your eyes of excellence and for viewing your editing as a ministry. I appreciate your God-centered care with this project.*

Last but not least:

- *My high school English teacher, Ms. Levyette (Furbert) Robinson, for your positive feedback about my poem. Our after-class conversation is still so vivid to me, and I have carried that inspiration from your classroom at The Berkeley Institute into every poem I later wrote. Thank you in every language!*

- *My accountability "angel," Michelle Lynn, literary agent with Christian Faith Publishing, who held me accountable for completing this project. Michelle, thank you for consistently checking in on the progress of my manuscript, which significantly helped me inch my way to the finish line. You played a bigger role than you probably even realize. Heartfelt thanks!*

- *All publishing company representatives who reviewed Rhyming with God. Although I partnered with Wipf and Stock Publishers to bring this project to print, I am grateful for the time you took to review my manuscript. Your feedback and interest in this project contributed to it reaching this stage. We all have a role to play on behalf of God's Kingdom—in Heaven and on Earth—so thank you for the role you played with Rhyming with God.*

"Just as our bodies have many parts and each part has a special function, so it is with Christ's body. We are many parts of one body, and we all belong to each other." Romans 12:4–5 (NLT)

During a retreat with Young Life Clay County board members, I learned about the thirty-day devotional *Being with Jesus* by Jim Branch and knew I had to get a copy. I began reading it at the start of the COVID-19 pandemic.

On day eighteen, the topic "When you pray" was explored. The prayer instructions were: "Use these verses in Matthew [6:5–15] to guide your prayer time today. Find a quiet place, go into the room of your soul, and shut the door. Just spend some time being with God. Utter whatever words rise in your heart. Finish your time of prayer by saying the Lord's Prayer. Pray it slowly, pausing to reflect, or linger, as God leads."[1]

Here are the words I uttered as they rose in my heart:

ENTER THE ROOM

I enter the room of my soul and close the door
Seeking God to heal and cure
To shine His grace upon this land
To remind us that it's on His love we depend

Lift us up, God
Hear our cry

1. Branch, *Being with Jesus*, 101.

Shake this world
To in You abide

Forgive our sins and dust us off
Help us to seek You
Before we take off
With our own plans and that of man

Fill our tanks with Your grace
Love, peace, and joy for every race
Love our neighbors as ourselves
Run this race, and run it well

May we seek You for health of all kinds
Realizing that prayer intimacy with You
Was ordained since
The beginning of time.

In Jesus' Name,
Amen.

Easily moved to tears and to words that rhyme, this tearful expression flowed from me immediately after watching a powerful video of a mother and daughter dancing during a peaceful protest. "My Tears Are the Cries of My Ancestors" is a tribute to my beloved ancestors, who helped pave the way for the life in God I live today.

MY TEARS ARE THE CRIES OF MY ANCESTORS

My tears are the cries of my ancestors
Who prayed to be free
Yet the day they prayed for
Many never got to see

My tears are the cries of my ancestors
Who labored all day long
Body feeling tired
But spirit staying strong

My tears are the cries of my ancestors
From whom my family came to be
Without God and our beloved ancestors
This life we wouldn't get to see

My tears are the cries of my ancestors
Whose spirits are now free
As they whisper from Heaven
"Go forth and keep fighting for what we didn't get to see!"

In Freedom with God,
Amen.

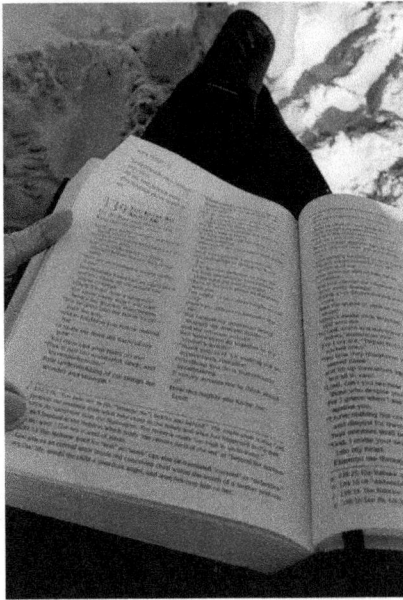

As I prepared for a fall cleanse on October 26, 2022, I sensed words wanting to pour onto the page during my devotional time. God held my hand, and "Temple of the Holy Spirit" flowed from my pen.

TEMPLE OF THE HOLY SPIRIT

The body as the temple of the Holy Spirit is on my mind
Deeply divine, a one-of-a-kind design

God's light radiating into it
Taking plentiful time with God to sit

Luke 17:21 teaches us "the Kingdom of God is within"
So, shouldn't we aim to keep the body healthy, holy, and free from sin?

Viewing it from a godly perspective
Taking time to be spiritually connected

Drinking both the Word and water to hydrate
Putting healthy food on our spiritual and physical plates

Loving each other, as God lives in us
Aiming to live our days with pure love and no fuss

Thinking *What would Jesus do?* before we proceed
Respecting each other, planting good seeds

Exercising for a healthy heart, strong bones, clear mind, and flexibility
Providing our temples with great strength and agility

Not for reasons of vanity
Nor to impress humanity

Rather, because the body is the temple of the Holy Spirit of God living in us
And isn't that enough reason to treat the body—the temple—with respect and trust?

Poetic Movement, Embodied Worship, Devotion in Motion

Embodied worship on the mat. Photo courtesy of Javi Fernandez, owner of Dance4Life, Fleming Island, FL.

I love to praise and worship God with my entire being—body, mind, soul, and spirit.

While I have loved and worshiped God for as long as I can remember, once I began adding physical movement to my devotional time, my relationship with my Creator shifted to new levels.

I have prayerfully shared "On the Mat" and "Thank You, Jesus" to encourage you to connect with God in an embodied way.

ON THE MAT

When I encountered God on my exercise mat
I also met His kinesthetic intellect
Moving through my body, mind, soul, and spirit
God expressed Himself to me in a way I could hear Him

No clue I would meet God in this way
As He revealed Himself to me that Tuesday
Life became a brand new day
Enhancing my journey and the way I pray

This time with God on the mat
Reminds me how much He has my back
Whether standing, sitting, supine, or prone
God assures me I'm one of His own

The closeness with Him can't be denied
On my mat, I've smiled and cried
Tears of joy and spiritual intimacy
Because when on the mat, it's purely God and me!

In Meeting God on the Mat,
Amen.

THANK YOU, JESUS

In Your peace on my sacred mat
Is where we meet and soulfully connect
Raising my arms and stretching toward the floor
I closely feel Your presence, which I adore

Thank You, Jesus, for meeting me on the mat
Thank You for holding me when I rest on my back
Thank You for Your grace and loving ways
Thank You for Your presence all of my days

The yawns I take on the mat with watery eyes
Releasing stress and internal cries
Letting go of what won't serve me throughout the day
As I fill up with You and follow Your way.

In Your Precious Name, I pray,
Amen.

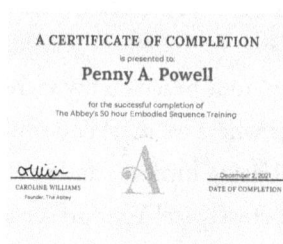

As a Christ-centered embodied movement teacher, I enrolled in the fifty-hour Christ-centered Embodied Sequence Training led by The Abbey in 2021. During the journaling segments of this online training, poetic writing often poured out of me. I was blessed to share the poems with the class participants and leaders, who were so encouraging about the rhyming expressions, often requesting to hear more. I have included six of those inspired poems on the following pages.

LETTING GO

I let go of the stress of the day
Meeting Jesus on my mat
Surrendering His way

I enter His presence
Giving Him my mind, body, soul, and spirit
In His love, I move
From His grace, I release any heaviness I carry

Letting go of the tension of the day
I meet Jesus on my mat
Embracing our peaceful date
As He fills my sacred cup and plate.

In Letting Go,
Amen.

DEAR EVER-PRESENT GOD,

Surrendered, open
Feeling free
Loved, peaceful
Allowed to be me

Movement, stillness
Quiet peace
Spiritual guidance
An inner retreat

Holding stress
Letting go
Releasing it all
From You, I flow

From Your heart
To my mat
Meeting You
With no regret

This is the path
You've carved for me
May I meet it
With pure integrity

Your love in my bones
So I'm never alone
Led by Your care
I know You are near . . .

You are here!

In Your Presence,
Amen.

DEAR LOVING GOD,

Tears flowing from this space
As I look in the 'mirror'
I see Your face
Your robe
Your hand
Extended to me
In Your grace is where I want to be

Arms stretched wide
Nothing for me to hide
You by my side
In for a divine ride

Love, joy, and peace, I taste
You, Jesus, are in this holy place
As I move at Your pace
Within this space
With You always, I will run this race.

In Your Love,
Amen.

DEAR POETIC GOD,

I meet You through poetry on my mat yet again
My Lord, My Redeemer, My Maker, My Friend
You and Your goodness have no end
You, Jesus, are always lovingly in command

You have my heart
And my soul
I see You; I greet You
In Your Name, I am bold

Lifted by Your hand
Guided by Your grace
Always and forever
You are in this space

Of love, healing, mercy, and light
You, O Jesus, sweetly fill my sight
In You, I delight
In You, the way is bright.

In Your Poetry,
Amen.

God's art on display during a getaway in Jekyll Island, GA, in 2019.

DEAR RADIANT ONE,

Blessed are You, O Radiant One
Shining brighter than Your morning sun
Creating an ocean of love for us to meet
In this space, we connect and greet

You take my hand
We swim about
Kept afloat by You
I have no doubt

Ocean waves
Moving through space
God, it's You
You are in this place

The appearance of waves
Even on my mat
I explore with You
As we deeply connect

Holy of Holies
Held on high
Shining brighter
Than Your beautiful night sky

Magnificent turquoise ocean
Is what I see
Lord, O Lord
Connected with me

Swimming in Your love
Floating in Your grace
Holy of Holies
You've created this space

In this space
I swim with You
As You hold my hand
And guide me through

Flowing freely as we swim about
Lord, with You there is no self-doubt
An ocean of love beyond compare
My Maker, My Creator—You are here!

Captured by Your Love
Whole and free
Lord, O Lord
You are swimming with me

In awe of You
Held on high
A divine encounter
In the ocean sky.

In Your Radiance,
Amen.

"Those who look to him for help will be radiant with joy . . ."
Psalm 34:5 (NLT)

BOLD IN CHRIST

Taking inventory of my soul
Things of new and of old
Stories shared, some left untold
Strong, new, energized, and bold

Bold in Christ
Who fills my cup
Strengthens my spirit
And lifts me up

Beyond the world
Peace assured
Hope in Him
God's love adored.

In Boldness with Christ,
Amen.

Poetic Workouts

Planking as I pray.

Working out is a hobby of mine. I am grateful that I enjoy exercising because I see physical movement as a gift from God to benefit the body, mind, soul, and spirit. I call it *natural medicine.*

I enjoy the gift of movement so much that I have taught a faith-based class, *Stretch, Strengthen, and Relax,* for many years in my community. I also have the wonderful opportunity to guide beloved seniors—who are members of Uniper Care—with movement by virtually teaching *Body Balance.* Additionally, I facilitate an interactive class, *Golden Moments of Gratitude.*

The poetic expression "Camp Gladiator" flowed from me after a 5 a.m. workout in the great outdoors (a parking lot). It was led by my dear trainer and friend, Terie Wanger, who taught many early-morning outdoor workouts, which allowed me to get solid movement and fresh air before going to the workplace during that season of life. Terie now offers these workouts virtually at various times. Meet her at www.bodybyterie.com.

As we mature mentally and spiritually, it's important that we also grow in physical strength because our body is the temple of the Holy Spirit (1 Cor 6:19).

Sweat and smiles in my CG shirt after a virtual CG workout.

CAMP GLADIATOR

This morning's Camp Gladiator workout
Sweat from head to toe
And to think
I almost didn't go

I looked at the clock
And figured it was too late
But a feeling took over
To still make it to my 5 a.m. CG date

Peak Week workout sequences a bit more intense
Equipping the body to build strength and defense
Helping us to be healthy and strong
As we CG campers say, "CG strong all day long!"

My face was dripping
My clothes were drenched
Which felt detoxifying, purifying
With no denying

That whether there's a spark or sigh in our eyes
Depending on the exercise
Each CG workout is a special surprise
And the power of exercise just never lies.

"So whether you eat or drink or whatever you do, do it all for the glory of God." 1 Cor 10:31 (NIV)

Poetic Encounters with "The Time ReDesign"

Reflecting while bundled up in my husband's jacket on a cold day
on St. Simons Island, GA, on the eve of Resurrection Sunday 2023.

Do you take time to step away from the demands of life *to just be*
with God?

During Lent 2023, I participated in *The Time ReDesign*, a
program created and facilitated by Etta Hornsteiner, ICF™ board-
certified integrative health and wellbeing coach-practitioner,
educator, speaker, and author of *Ten Guiding Lights to Health and
Wholeness*. The program explored *chronos* (linear) time versus
kairos (God's timing) and the ways we can adjust our lives and use
contemplative practices to live in closer rhythm with God.

As was the case during my training journey with The Abbey, poetry flowed from me during my participation in *The Time ReDesign*. From "Slowing Down" to "The Impact of Thoughts on Time," these poems unfolded as Etta led us deeper into the redesign of time.

If you'd also like to go deeper in your time with God in a "transformational group coaching" setting, Etta is an anointed teacher and facilitator, "bridging Christian spirituality and behavorial change." Meet her at www.liveliving.org.

SLOWING DOWN WITH GOD

God, slowing down with You
Is the best thing to do

Resting in Your love
Centered in Your grace
O, Dear God, You move us out of the rat race

In Your will
Heart filled
Joy to spill

God, slowing down with You
Is the most precious thing to do!

In Slowing Down,
Amen.

DEAR NOURISHING GOD,

Not based on chronos time
Your path is eternal, blessed, and beautifully divine
One of a kind
Nourishment for the body, soul, spirit, and mind

You are far more than time
Easy to find

If . . .

We seek You with heart and soul
Prayers bold
Spirit hot, not cold
Whether young or old
You are the mold
NOT time!

So why do we prioritize and glorify time
Instead of You, The Eternal Divine?

Time has become the idol
God, please set us free
Shift us to focus on You
And what You see
Which is life in You, eternally!

In Your Nourishment,
Amen.

During *The Time ReDesign* program, we were taught how to use breathing to align the body with the rhythm of Scripture verses. For instance, I chose Psalm 150:6 (NIV) as my breath scripture—"Let everything that has breath praise the LORD." As I inhaled, I internally said, *"Let everything that has breath . . . "* Then, as I exhaled, I internally said, *"Praise the LORD."*

We were invited to use this breathing exercise in the evening to ponder two questions: "Who am I being? Who am I becoming?"[2] I went to bed that night inhaling and exhaling these questions.

I awoke the next morning with four rhythmic lines in my head, so I jumped out of bed to get the words on paper, as I sensed this was the start of something more. The following poem then unfolded in its fullness.

WHO AM I BEING? WHO AM I BECOMING?

It's a song
A poem
You're coming into your own
With Me

Watch the pattern
The rhythm
The shape
The form
This is what you've been becoming
Since you were born

Look at what's mattered most
During the first half of your life

2. Hornsteiner, "The Time ReDesign."

We're now shaping these elements
And making them tight

Tightening up the first half
For you to live even closer to Me
That's who you're becoming
That's who you'll be

The daughter of mine
You were born to be
All of you
All of Me
Penny and God
For eternity

Watch the patterns
Watch the design
It's all My rhythm
It's all in My time

Your life will flourish
More with The Divine
Like Etta said,
"From grapes to wine."

This is your journey
With your time redesign!

Amen.

Later in *The Time ReDesign*, we were asked to reflect on our discovery of slowing down our breathing. This time, I used Psalm 46:10 (NLT) as my breath prayer to breathe more slowly:

Inhale: "*Be still,*"

Exhale: "*and know that I am God!*"

My discovery was the following poem, "Slowing Down the Breath," which was not written in rhyme. In addition to helping us live deeper with God, slower breathing has various physical benefits, such as reducing anxiety and blood pressure. I encourage you to research this subject. I am reading *Breath as Prayer* by Jennifer Tucker, which I was excited to find in Publix, my local grocery store.

SLOWING DOWN THE BREATH

As I slow down my breathing
My body becomes calmer and my mind quieter
Internal space expands
Increasing my awareness of God in me

At times, these deeper, conscious breaths
Evoke big yawns and watery eyes
A sense of deep releasing, cleansing
A shift into deeper layers of peace and balance

External elements drift away
As I experience what feels like *floating* with God in space
My awareness of our connection
Deepens and strengthens

Slowing down my breathing, I become more centered
And present with my Creator
As I breathe with Him, sit with Him, stretch with Him, relax with Him
Meditate on Him, and be still with Him

Slowing down my breathing
Sets me up for healthy rest
In the vast love
And peace of God

Slowing down my breathing
Allows me to breathe a sacred rhythm
Of wholesome rest
It's timeless
It's pure
It's the best!

In Slowing Down the Breath,
Amen.

Although slowing down our breathing is beneficial for various reasons, the mind, however, can get distracted when meditating on God and His Word. In *The Time ReDesign*, we learned that selecting a sacred word, focusing on it, and practicing contemplative sacred breathing help to remove the distractions. My word choice was "anchor," which effectively altered my rhythm.

ANCHOR

I felt anchored by God
And rooted in His love
Held by His grace
Enjoying this wonderful taste
Of His Presence
Nestled
Hopeful
Feeling free
Grateful
Renewed
Rooted like a tree
And ready to explore
The deeper waters of God and me!

SACRED WORD BREATHING

Integrating a sacred word with my breathing
Added power to my lungs
Strengthened my mind
And brought me closer to The Divine

It also helped to produce this rhyme
Revealing the power of Kairos time
Demonstrating what happens when we combine
The beauty of breathing with God's Word
And connecting with the love and peace of being heard . . .
By Him!

"What are the familiar negative or not-so-positive thoughts that impact how you use time? How do these thoughts keep you stuck?"[3]

These important questions were the final reflections from *The Time ReDesign* program, and I struggled to compose my answers. My written answers would not flow, so I prayed for God to take hold of my thoughts and keyboard, and He inspired me in poetic form once again.

THE IMPACT OF THOUGHTS ON TIME

Are you stuck in time?

Living in the past in my mind
Therefore, staying stuck in old time
Ruminating on what has passed
That wasn't intended to last

Desiring to recreate what has gone
From the experiences that were long ago born
Perhaps holding on to what was already enjoyed and learned
Which now needs to be let go of, buried, or burned

Since I don't always elevate my thinking above how I feel
I'm, unfortunately, making my brain deal
With things of old that have passed away
And not fully opening myself to a whole new way

This, then, keeps me stuck
Putting undue pressure on my brain
Keeping some areas of life stale and the same
Where needing to retrain and create a new lane

3. Hornsteiner, "The Time ReDesign."

To more fluidly flow with The One I love
Our good and precious God above
To places and spaces unimagined
Around Heaven on Earth
In the greatness and fullness of my God-given worth!

In Living Unstuck,
Amen.

Resurrection Weekend 2023

The peaceful grounds of Epworth By The Sea, St. Simons Island, GA.

It was 5:50 on a rainy Resurrection Sunday morning in 2023, and I was at Epworth By The Sea, a Christian property located on St. Simons Island, Georgia. I felt led to retreat at this sanctuary to begin wrapping up *Rhyming with God* while also exploring St. Simons Island with my husband, Collin.

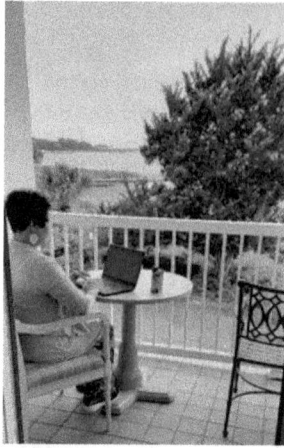

Moments after entering our hotel room, I spotted a framed poem hanging on the wall and sensed it was a sign from God confirming I was exactly where He led me to be, as I had not even heard about this property until moments before booking the trip.

I quickly set up my workspace on the balcony to begin fine-tuning my manuscript. I was blessed with a peaceful view of the Frederica River and the sounds of a church bell and instrumental hymns that could be heard approximately every 15 minutes. I knew I was on holy ground.

Prayer tower at Epworth By The Sea

The next day, Resurrection Sunday, Collin and I visited the prayer tower, where the church bell was located. It was a special experience to step inside this structure to pray.

As we walked the grounds, Collin spotted a poem written on a memorial stone in loving memory of a poet. "Penny, come see this!" he called out to me. Excitedly reading the poem, I knew it was another sign from God to complete and share *Rhyming with God.*

During the wee hours of Resurrection Sunday, after engaging in a devotional related to Psalm 139 and a creative contemplation about St. Julian of Norwich, both by leaders of The Abbey, I wrote "Don't Lose Sight of God's Love."

DON'T LOSE SIGHT OF GOD'S LOVE

St. Julian of Norwich said many years ago,
"My, how busy we become
when we lose sight of how God loves us."

Today, we still fill our days with fuss and rush
From here to there as if it's all a great must
Often overlooking the One we most need
Forgetting to pause, surrender, relax, and take heed

May we step back from this pace
And take time away from the rat race
To readjust our sight
And connect with God's might

Whether day or night
His way is right
His path is bright
Sacred and a delight

May we connect with Him
Be free from sin
Honoring Kairos time
And how God rhymes

In this way, it becomes both prayer and sacred play
Aligned with God without delay
A sweet exploration of abundant love
With our great and precious God above.

In Rhythm with God,
Amen.

Simple Poetic Prayers from My Journal

I've penned several poems in my copy of *Women Finding God: Prayer Journal.* Two of these are "Rest & Reset" and "Dear Healing God." While "Rest & Reset" was written long before I participated in *The Time ReDesign,* the poem reminds me of our group discussion about the importance of Sabbath rest and its healing properties.

REST & RESET

Dear God,

Thank You for this day of rest
A day to reset and never forget
You are on the throne
And I am one of Your own

You pick me up
And dust me off
Healing my body, soul, spirit, and mind
Reminding me that I'm one of a kind

Created by You
You reveal to me what to do
Because without You
I don't have a clue

Please bless my family and friends today
Increase the time with You, we rest and pray
Thank You for Your forgiveness, love, and grace
And for helping us to live according to Your peaceful pace.

In Resting & Resetting,
Amen.

DEAR HEALING GOD,

Please give us:

Empathy and compassion
Love and grace
Peace and kindness
And a healthy pace

Love and light
Endurance and truth
With a clear understanding
That You're the root

Please forgive worldwide hurt
And heal the pain
Help us to live in unity
In Jesus' Name.

Amen.

"Devotional Writer," which I journaled in 2021, became a prayer answered in 2022. Since then, some of the devotions I have written have been published on ChristianDevotions.us.[4]

Another devotion, "Silence, Sweet Silence," was included in the Summer 2024 edition of *The Secret Place: Devotions for Daily Worship*, published by Judson Press.

DEVOTIONAL WRITER

A devotional writer, I will be
Writing for the Kingdom of Christ
Communicating thoughts from God
With vigor and delight

"Leveling up," my sister Takiyah says
Elevating my writing
Words unfolding
That are spiritually inviting

Embracing this sacred time with God
Who shares thoughts with me as a friend
As I write about His love
And a world without end

A legacy of uplifting communication
I pray for my devotional writing to be
On behalf of the Kingdom of God
For my beloved family, friends, and community!

In Writing with God,
Amen.

4. https://christiandevotions.us/viewauthor/5764.

Family Tributes

Playing in the snow in Virginia Beach, VA, in 1998
with my then toddler son, Caleb.

My deepest calling has been that of motherhood. My son, Caleb, is now a grown young man, but praying parents never stop praying for God's hand upon our children.

It's fun to share here that when my son was in elementary school, one of his poems was selected for publication in the 2008 edition of *Anthology of Poetry by Young Americans*. He also wrote a poem—"The Night Sky"—for a class assignment, which beautifully demonstrated his poetic ability. I greatly appreciated those opportunities to witness Caleb's poetic skill; however, unlike my passion for words, his is numbers.

I penned "Poetic Motherhood" to thank God for my son's life and the gift of motherhood. You, too, can pray this poetic prayer by inserting your children's names.

Dinner in Jacksonville, FL, in 2023 with my now adult son, Caleb.

POETIC MOTHERHOOD

Dear God,

Thank you for the opportunity to be a mother
A calling for me like none other
The gift of a son, *Caleb Sekou*
Whom I pray will always walk closely with You

Thank You for Your protection upon his walk
For hearing his prayers when to You he talks
For placing Your Holy Spirit deeply in him
And for teaching him that it's with Jesus, we win

Thank You for also reminding him that it's You and family first
And it's for You, we must foremost thirst
For showing him there's a divine order in life
That helps us avoid unnecessary strife

Thank you for the hands-on example of my mother to me
Then, to *Caleb*, a loving and dedicated mother I knew to be
From my mother, grandmothers, aunts, godmothers, mother-in-law, friends, and all
I forever stand on their shoulders and gratefully embrace this motherhood call.

In Motherhood,
Amen.

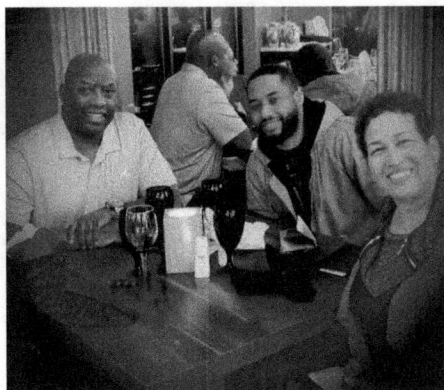

Family dinner outing in Jacksonville, FL, 2023.

When my son turned twenty-five (he's older now), I wrote "Dear Son" as a birthday tribute to him. As the words poured out, so did the abundance of gratitude in my heart.

DEAR SON,

Twenty-five years ago
Your dad and I were given a calling
To raise a young man
A sacred assignment we'd do again and again

That calling was to raise you
To spread your wings
To use your voice
To make a good choice

To be kind to others
To make a difference from your heart
Oh, how blessed we were
For the opportunity to nurture your start

My husband and son taking in the scenery after a boat ride during a family outing to Okefenokee Swamp Park in GA in March 2011.

So, today as I reflect
I deeply thank God for placing us on this parenting track
An invaluable journey of love, purpose, lessons, laughs, and tears
Varied emotions with some based on human fears

Through it all, we've been reminded to surrender to God
Our Beloved Creator, Sustainer, and Friend
To the One who richly blessed us
With parenting love that could never end

Thank You, Thank You, Dear God
For showing us the parenting way
It was a joy to point Caleb to You
Each and every day

I pray that his eyes remain fixed on You
For all of his life
And if it be Your Will
He'll one day lead children and a wife

May Caleb follow Your divine design
Every step of the way
Thy Will be done
And in Jesus' Name, we pray.

Amen.

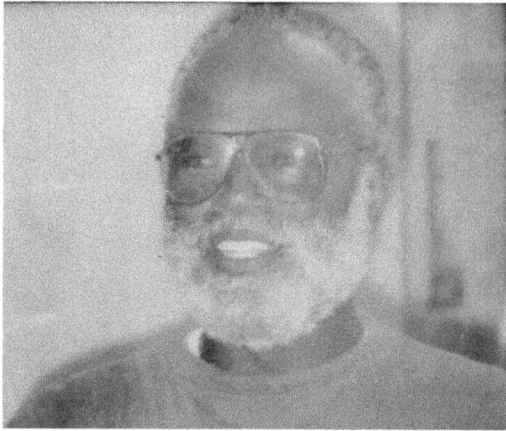

My beloved father, Ainsworth "Kebede" Burgess

While I am blessed to still have my mom, Caroline Burgess, in my life, my dad, Ainsworth "Kebede" Burgess, was called to eternal rest in 1996, when my son was only five months old. Over the years, I've written several poetic tributes in memory of my dad. "Dear Daddy" was written on the twenty-fifth anniversary of his transition to the Arms of our Savior.

DEAR DADDY,

Time moves quickly
Yet our precious memories remain
Daddy, we will always love and miss you
And continue to speak and cherish your name

Twenty-five years ago
You were laid to rest
Leaving us with a legacy
That we consider the absolute best

A legacy of love, faith, hope, joy
Wisdom, and peace
The spiritual foundation you provided
Could never be beat

Thank you for this and all that you were
And although we wish you were still here
We know that God called you there
But your voice we still hear
And your love we will always share

We love you forever and ever!

In Loving Memory,
Amen.

Flanked by my parents, Ainsworth and Caroline Burgess, my brother, Jude, and sister, Takiyah, at my graduation in 1988 from Simmons College in Boston, MA. Other beloved family members can be seen in the background.

Working and Flowing
with God's Direction

A beautiful mug gifted to me by a former coworker at St. Johns River State College (SJR State).

I was reflecting on my workweek one day during my former employment as a communications specialist in the Office of Public Relations at SJR State, and "Gratitude" flowed from my heart.

GRATITUDE

The end of a week
Feeling peaceful and strong
Thanking the Good Lord
For His love and grace all week long

Nestled at home
With a cup of herbal tea
Reflecting on the workweek
And the words I got to speak . . .

Through the writing I did
In my role at work
Arranging words most days
Definitely feels like a perk

I've had this thing with words
Since I was young
Putting them together
Has always been joyful and fun

As I reflect on this process
And the work that I do
"Yes, you get to play with words"
Is the message that comes through

While no situation is perfect
And elements can sometimes feel out of place
When I reflect on my work
I clearly see God's love and grace

The hand of God present
In all that I do
No doubt, it is my Creator
Who equips me and gets me through

Every piece of an article
A press release or poem
Yes, I do love to write
But the words are never my own

Humble enough to know
God gives me the words to express
And because of that
I'll always be writing my best.

In Gratitude,
Amen.

After finishing my almost seven-year employment at SJR State, I wrote "My Why" as a prayer for clarity about my next step. I was eager to stay in rhythm with God's plan for the upcoming chapter of my career journey, which ended up being a virtual support and customer service role with the Christ-centered wellness company, Limbic System Rewire (LSR). Managing LSR's virtual support desk, I was able to once again use my enjoyment of writing.

The steps of my transition are depicted in the poems, "What Am I to Do?," which poured out of me during a morning devotional study of Genesis 1; "Prayers for the Prison Fellowship Ministry"; and the devotion article "Bittersweet." But, first, "My Why."

MY WHY

I speak, I teach, I write
Through a voice
Given to me
To glorify God

This is my why
This is my high
This is my cry
God in me, I will never deny

Equipped in God's love
Prepared by divine grace
I stand in victory in God
Prayerfully moving at His pace

Out of the rat race
Living mindfully in my space
God, please keep holding my hand
And shining Your love on my face.

In Your Purpose,
Amen.

WHAT AM I TO DO?

Today, I ask the questions:
God, what am I to do?
What is my ultimate career responsibility
Perfectly designed by You?

Please lead me to that role, Lord
Show me Your way
For living in the fullness of Your glory
Each and every day

Please give me the clarity
To step up to the plate
Not a moment before
And not a moment too late

I yearn to write of You
With fullness of heart
From You, I want to express
And give my writing the absolute best

Please lead me to the waters, Lord
From which I should drink
Take me away from anything
That makes my writing shrink

You put the pen in my hand, God
So it's surely not from man
Please show me where to best use it and never abuse it
Where to create and not disintegrate

In Genesis 1
You show us Your power to create
From that power, I move
Ready to step up to the plate

The plate of my newest role
Of which I am well paid
Work highly valued
Never a slave . . .

To any thought process
That goes against Your way
For it's in You, I strive
From the words You say.

In Jesus' Name, I pray,
Amen.

Before working with LSR, I applied for a writing and editing position with Prison Fellowship. By the grace of God, I was shortlisted out of over 200 applicants, making it to the final few being considered for this role. Although the job turned out to be for someone else, I thoroughly enjoyed the interview process, which included an interesting editing and writing assignment that I was given days to work on.

A poetic prayer poured out of me on the day of my first interview, and I continue to pray for this ministry. As Hebrews 13:3 (ESV) teaches us, "Remember those who are in prison, as though in prison with them, and those who are mistreated, since you also are in the body."

PRAYERS FOR THE PRISON FELLOWSHIP MINISTRY

Dear God,

If it is Your will
May I serve with the Prison Fellowship ministry
Honoring Your call "to remember those in prison"
By writing and editing to help with this mission

Helping the incarcerated
Including their children
Every one
Of the "nearly 1.5 million"[5]

5. Prison Fellowship, "Reconciling Families to Break the Cycle of Incarceration," para. 1.

Writing to bring awareness
And favor and engagement to this cause
Sharing hope with our brothers and sisters
Who have gotten lost

Replacing the cycle of brokenness
With love, prison reform, and openness
Strengthening bonds between children and their parents behind bars
Promoting the need for transformation to remove the scars

May I use the abilities You have given me in communications
To help prisoners live according to Your foundation
With faith, hope, love, and dedication
Helping us work with You to bring healing to this nation

Calling the Church to help lead the way
Guiding our prisoners to a brighter day
A prisoner at a time—a nation restored
Families strengthened—God adored

Hope unleashed
The incarcerated living in God's love and peace
Please equip me well for the job ahead
From Your breath and voice
May the Prison Fellowship programs continue to be led

Position me, Dear Lord, to support the mission
Serving as Your hands and feet to uplift the human condition
Sharing the message of You, Dear Jesus, and Your never-ending grace
May You help us to help those in need
As they come to know You—face to face.

In Your Name, I pray.

Thank You, God!

Amen.

Bittersweet: A Devotion

> So I went to the angel and said to him, "Give me the little book." And he said to me, "Take and eat it; and it will make your stomach bitter, but it will be as sweet as honey in your mouth" (Revelation 10:9, OSB).

As we know, the roads of life come with twists and turns. As we're traveling along these winding roads, we can encounter the sweet, the bitter, and the sweet again, just as we can in God's Word.

According to *The Orthodox Study Bible* (study notes about Revelation 10:8–11), "The symbolism of eating refers to receiving a revelation from God . . . The contrast between sweetness in the mouth and bitterness in the stomach shows the sweetness of receiving God's revelation (announcing God's victory for His people) as opposed to the bitterness of its message of woe (announcing God's terrible judgments, as well as sufferings for His faithful ones)."

This notion of *sweet and bitter* brings a personal experience to mind.

During my job search process, I was offered a remote position as a marketing content specialist with a college ranked one of the best for spiritual development. My Zoom interview was with the Marketing and Communications (MarCom) team members, and we connected so well. A few days later, on a Saturday, I received the call I had been waiting for—the job was mine!

However, the following week, the college's MarCom director was the bearer of news neither of us had wanted to hear. Turns out, this college was not licensed to hire remote employees from Florida, so my opportunity to work with this talented team was gone—just like that! Although saddened, I knew God would soon flavor the bitterness with His sweetness.

Weeks later, I received a heartwarming card in the mail from the MarCom director noting that I was in his thoughts and prayers. When I sent him a thank-you text, he replied, "I can honestly say I miss working with you, even though we never got started!"

I felt the same.

Tasting the sweetness of what could have been, mixed with the bitterness of what didn't happen, I called my husband at work in bittersweet tears.

I later reached out to the director to let him know that things were going well. In his detailed reply, he even extended an invitation to my husband and me to stay at his and his wife's home should we ever visit their area. Deeply touched, I could hear my sister-in-law Rosalyn's words ringing in my ears, "God's sheep knows God's sheep!"

When the sweet road we're traveling suddenly meets a bitter intersection, may we not get stuck there. Rather, I pray we trust that God's hands will never leave the steering wheel, as He helps us navigate through the bitter and back to *Sweet Street*. And, who knows, we may even unleash some poetry or a devotional article along the way!

Bibliography

Branch, Jim. *Being with Jesus*. Middletown, DE: N.p., 2020.

Hornsteiner, Etta. "The Time ReDesign." https://liveliving.org/time.

Piper, John. "God Filled Your Bible with Poems." Aug 16, 2016. https://www. desiringgod.org/articles/god-filled-your-bible-with-poems.

Prison Fellowship. "Reconciling Families to Break the Cycle of Incarceration." https://www.prisonfellowship.org/2022/04/reconciling-families.

www.ingramcontent.com/pod-product-compliance
Lightning Source LLC
Chambersburg PA
CBHW061505040426
42450CB00008B/1491